THE ULTIMATE ANIMAL LIBRARY

Lemurs

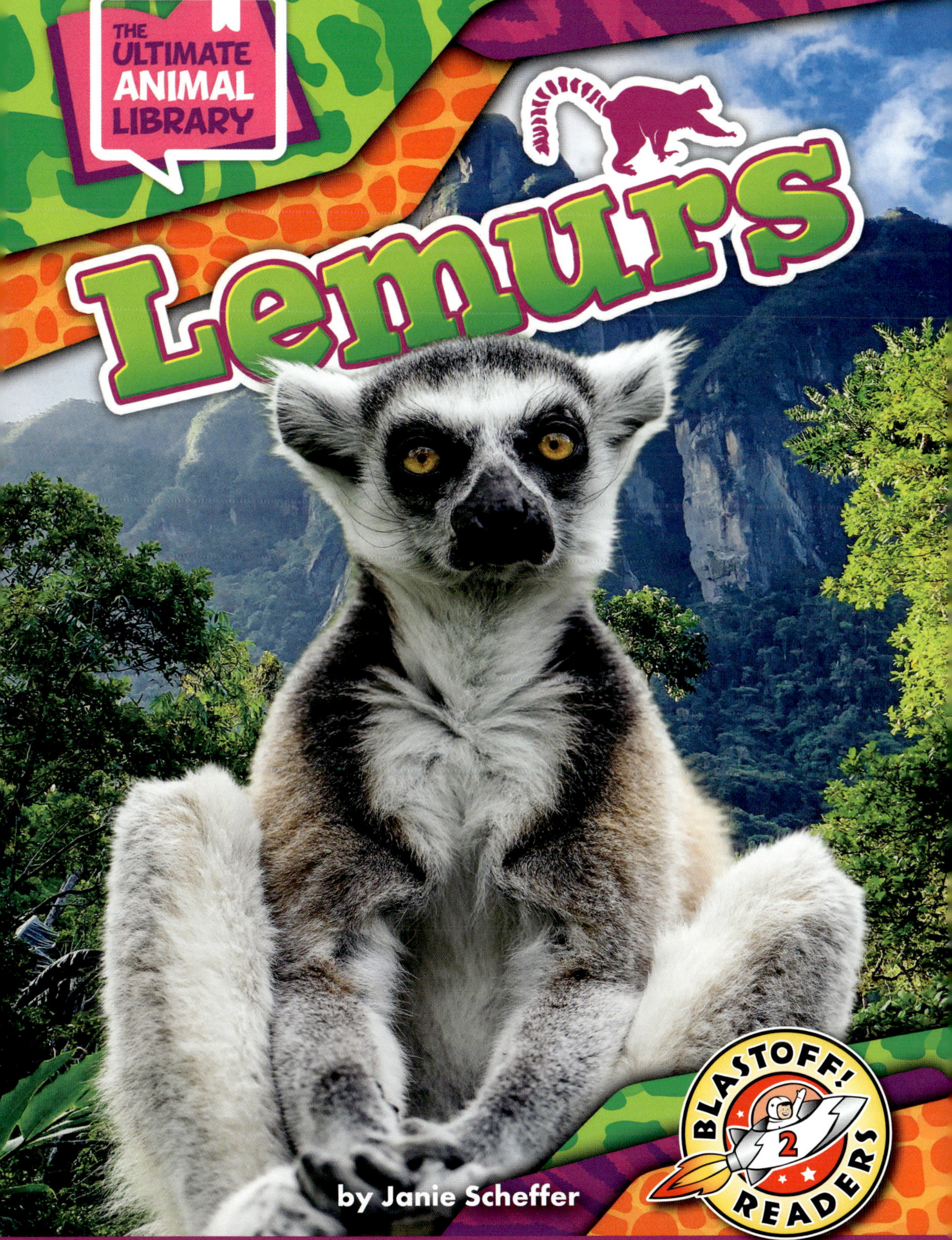

by Janie Scheffer

BLASTOFF! READERS 2

BLASTOFF! READERS, AN IMPRINT OF BELLWETHER MEDIA BY FLUTTERBEE

Blastoff! Readers are carefully developed by literacy experts to build reading stamina and move students toward fluency by combining standards-based content with developmentally appropriate text.

LEVELS

Level 1 provides the most support through repetition of high-frequency words, light text, predictable sentence patterns, and strong visual support.

Level 2 offers early readers a bit more challenge through varied sentences, increased text load, and text-supportive special features.

Level 3 advances early-fluent readers toward fluency through increased text load, less reliance on photos, advancing concepts, longer sentences, and more complex special features.

★ **Blastoff! Universe**

Reading Level

Blastoff! Beginners — Grade K

Blastoff! Readers — Grades 1–3

Blastoff! Discovery — Grade 4

This edition first published in 2027 by Bellwether Media, Inc.

Library of Congress Cataloging-in-Publication Data

Names: Scheffer, Janie, 1992- author
Title: Lemurs / by Janie Scheffer.
Description: Minneapolis, Minnesota : Bellwether Media, Inc., 2027. | Series: Ultimate animal library | Includes bibliographical references and index. | Audience: Ages 5-8 | Audience: Grades 2-3 | Summary: "Relevant images match informative text in this introduction to lemurs. Intended for students in kindergarten through third grade"-- Provided by publisher.
Identifiers: LCCN 2026013884 (print) | LCCN 2026013885 (ebook) | ISBN 9798898800413 (library binding) | ISBN 9798898801656 (ebook)
Subjects: LCSH: Lemurs
Classification: LCC QL737.P95 S36 2027 (print) | LCC QL737.P95 (ebook)
LC record available at https://lccn.loc.gov/2026013884
LC ebook record available at https://lccn.loc.gov/2026013885

Editor: Elizabeth Neuenfeldt Designer: Brittany McIntosh

Printed in the United States of America, North Mankato, MN.

Table of Contents

What Are Lemurs?

Lemurs are small **mammals**. There are more than 100 different kinds of lemurs! Most of these **primates** are found in Madagascar.

Ring-tailed Lemur Report

Range

Status in the Wild

Habitats

forests

scrublands

Lemurs have soft fur.
It can be brown, red,
gray, black, or white.

Most lemurs have big, round eyes.
They have **snouts** with wet noses.

Lemurs have five fingers on each hand. They have five toes on each foot.

Their hands and feet have pads. These help lemurs hold things.

Lemurs move on all fours. Some have longer back legs for jumping.

Most lemurs have tails. Some tails are long. They can be bushy. They can have stripes.

Spot a Lemur

A Troop!

Most lemurs live in forests.
Some live in **scrublands**.

They eat and sleep in trees. Some also live on the ground.

Some lemurs live in **troops**. Troops can have up to 30 lemurs. Troops are often led by females.

Troops work together to watch for **predators** and find food.

Some lemurs are active at night. Others are active during the day.

Some lemurs are **omnivores**. Others are **herbivores**.

Growing Up

Female lemurs give birth to one to six **infants** at a time. Infants **nurse**.

Most infants hug mom's belly for around two weeks. Then they ride on her back.

After one month, infants eat solid food. By six months, they can live on their own.

Lemurs can live for around 16 years!

Life of a Lemur

Name of Babies

infants

Number of Babies

1 to 6

Time Spent with Mom

around 6 months

Life Span

around 16 years

Glossary

herbivores—animals that only eat plants

infants—baby lemurs

mammals—warm-blooded animals that have backbones and feed their young milk

nurse—to drink mom's milk

omnivores—animals that eat both plants and animals

predators—animals that hunt other animals for food

primates—animals that use their hands to grasp food and other objects; primates are related to humans.

scrublands—dry lands that have mostly low plants and few trees

snouts—the noses and mouths of some animals

troops—groups of lemurs

To Learn More

AT THE LIBRARY

Becker, Trudy. *Lemurs.* Mendota Heights, Minn.: Apex, 2026.

Jaycox, Jaclyn. *Ring-tailed Lemur Princesses: Rulers of the Troop.* Mankato, Minn.: Pebble, 2022.

Rylands, Warren. *Ring-tailed Lemur.* New York, N.Y.: Lightbox Learning, 2025.

ON THE WEB

FACTSURFER

Factsurfer.com gives you a safe, fun way to find more information.

1. Go to www.factsurfer.com.
2. Enter "lemurs" into the search box and click 🔍.
3. Select your book cover to see a list of related content.

Index

The images in this book are reproduced through the courtesy of: Ondrej_Novotny_92, front cover (lemur), p. 4; Sean Newbery, front cover (background); Martin Pelanek, pp. 2-3; Eric Isselee, p. 3; Massimo Todaro, p. 6; Roberto Dani, p. 7; njaj, p. 8; tiverylucky, p. 9 (inset); GummyBone, p. 9; Natalia Paklina, pp. 10, 18; Pavel Kovacs, pp. 10-11; Logomaker691, p. 11; Rebel Red Runner, p. 12; StockMediaSeller, p. 13; Carl Jones Photography, p. 14; Peter Schaefer, p. 15; Foto-Jagla.de, pp. 16-17; Lubos Chlubny, p. 17 (fossa); Dirk M. de Boer, p. 17 (hawk); Martin Prochazkacz, p. 17 (boa constrictor); Goskova Tatiana, p. 17 (lemur); ibae.chatdanai, p. 17 (fruit); Mechanical Engineering, p. 17 (leaf); Artush, p. 17 (cicada); ptashkan, pp. 18-19; Denisapro, p. 20; Abeselom Zerit, p. 21; amine chakour, p. 22.